D0779150

Footsteps

PAMELA RUSHBY

Illustrated by Kevin Burgemeestre

Triple3Play

sundance
A Haights Cross Communications Company

Published by
Sundance Publishing
P.O. Box 740
One Beeman Road
Northborough, MA 01532

Copyright © text Pamela Rushby 1999
Copyright © illustrations Kevin Burgemeestre 1999

First published 1999 as Supa Dazzlers by
Addison Wesley Longman Australia Pty Limited
95 Coventry Street
South Melbourne 3205 Australia
Exclusive United States Distribution: Sundance Publishing

ISBN 0-7608-4798-3

Contents

Chapter 1

A House in the Country

"You've done *what?*" said Mom. She stopped stirring the spaghetti sauce and stared at Dad. Tom and Andy and I stopped doing our homework and stared at him, too.

"I've put a deposit on a house in the country," said Dad. "An old house in a small, quiet town. It's just the right spot for me to write my novel."

Tom and Andy and I looked at each other. We knew things were going to change when Dad lost his job at the newspaper. But we hadn't expected they would change this much.

"Don't you think," Mom said carefully to Dad, "we should have discussed this first?"

Dad looked surprised. "But we did," he said. "I told you I wasn't going to look for another job. I said I was going to write a book, and I needed peace and quiet to do it. I said we could move to the country."

"Well, yes," agreed Mom, "but I didn't think you meant right away."

"I did say I was going to talk to a real estate agent," said Dad.

That was true. Dad had said that. But somehow, none of us had believed it would ever happen. Now it had.

"There you are, then," said Dad. "I found the right place. We'll drive out to look at it on Saturday. Then we can move in almost right away. OK?" He left the kitchen and went down the hall.

"Well!" said Mom. She looked as if she
wanted to say a lot more. But she didn't.

"I don't believe this!" said Tom. Tom's my big
brother. He's sixteen.

"I'll have to change schools," said Andy.
Andy is my little sister. She's nine.

"I won't see my friends anymore!" I said. I'm Isabel. I'm thirteen.

"I'll have to give up my job," said Mom.

Then she looked at us seriously. "It's been hard for Dad, losing his job. You know that, don't you?" We knew. "Well, if this is what Dad thinks he needs, we should all be right behind him. Even if we have to change schools and friends—and jobs." Mom turned back to the spaghetti sauce. "It might not be so bad," she said. "We might like the country." She was trying hard to be cheerful, but I don't think she liked the idea much.

And we didn't like it at all.

We liked it even less when we drove out to the house on Saturday. The town was two hours out of the city. It was very small.

It had one grade school. No high school—
that was in the next town. A few stores. A
few new houses. A lot of old houses. And
our house was the oldest of all.

When we pulled up in front of it, even Dad
looked surprised. "It's the right street," he
said uncertainly, "and the right number. But
it looked a lot better in the real estate
photo."

"They always do," said Mom.

It was a big, two-story house. A porch edged with cast-iron rails ran all around the house. At one time it had probably been beautiful. Now the cast iron was rusty. The yard was overgrown. And one of the front steps was missing. While we watched, a bird flew out of a broken window.

"Can you get your deposit back?" asked Tom.

"Let's go inside!" said Dad heartily. "It might not be as bad as it seems." He pushed the gate open, and it fell off its hinges and crashed onto the walk.

"Bad omen," Tom whispered to me.

The house was every bit as bad inside as it was on the outside. Mom and Dad went from room to room. Dad pointed out the high ceilings, the wide windows, and the big rooms. Mom looked at the rusty sink, the broken floorboards, and the peeling paint. She looked more and more depressed.

Tom and Andy and I couldn't stand it anymore. We went outside and leaned on the car.

"Do you think it's really going to happen?" I asked.

"Can't miss," said Tom. "Dad's dead set on it. And Mom just wants to keep him happy. Face it. We're doomed."

"Doomed would be about right," said a voice.

Chapter 2

Horrible Things Happen There

We swung around. A girl about Tom's age was standing behind us, leaning on a bike. She had a big German shepherd dog with her.

"You're not moving in there, are you?" asked the girl. "Not in that house?"

"Why not?" said Tom. "Who's telling us we can't?" He wasn't having any local kid telling us what to do.

"I'm Jenna Daylight," said the girl.

"No one's lived in that house for twenty years. And there's a reason for that." She looked at Andy.

Andy's eyes had grown big and scared. Andy's nine, but she's little and skinny, so she looks younger. The girl had picked on her on purpose. She was trying to frighten Andy.

"Everyone knows," the girl said, "that house is haunted."

"Haunted!" Tom and I hooted. "Get out of here!"

The girl was still watching Andy. "Oh, yes, it is," she said. "Horrible things happen there."

"What—what sort of things?" asked Andy.

"Oh, things," said the girl. "Faces at the window. Howls in the night. Those sort of things."

Andy looked at us. "I don't want to live here!" she said.

Tom was angry. "Shut up!" he said to Jenna. "There's no such thing as ghosts! And we'll live here if we want to!"

"Suit yourself," said the girl. "Just trying to help. Come on, Alexander!" She called her dog and rode away.

Mom and Dad came out of the house. Dad looked down the street after the girl and her dog. "That's great!" he said. "Making friends already, eh?"

Tom and I looked at each other. "Something like that," I said.

"So," said Dad, "what do you think of your new home?"

We told him. It took quite a long time.

"And we absolutely, positively, definitely don't want to move!" we finished.

And so, of course, we moved.

The very next week we followed the big moving van all the way from the city, and pulled up outside the house. The moving men stared. "You sure this is it?" they asked.

"This is it, all right," we said.

"OK," said the men. "If you say so. Where do you want everything?"

Mom and Dad went ahead to open the doors. Mom went inside. "Oh, NO!" we heard her yell.

"Your mom hasn't been here before, then?" asked the men kindly.

We raced into the house. It had looked bad before, but it looked worse now. There was graffiti all over the walls—KEEP OUT! WARNING! HAUNTED!

"It'll take ages to clean this!" Dad groaned. But after the first shock, Mom didn't really seem to care. "What's one more thing to clean?" she said. "But who did it? And why?"

"Vandals, I suppose," fumed Dad. But Tom and Andy and I wondered.

It was dark by the time the house was even close to livable. Andy had quietly fallen asleep in a chair.

"Hungry, kids?" said Mom to Tom and me. We certainly were.

"Mom and I will go get pizzas," said Dad.

"You kids stay here and keep an eye on Andy, OK?"

"Sure," Tom and I said.

"Maybe," said Dad hopefully, "you could make a start on the graffiti while we're gone?"

"Don't count on it," we said.

Mom and Dad drove off. Andy heard the car leave and woke up. We looked at the graffiti, but we were too tired to start cleaning it.

After a few minutes, we noticed it was very quiet outside—very quiet and very dark. We weren't used to things being so quiet.

Andy looked nervously at the windows. The curtains weren't up yet. I think we were all remembering what Jenna had said about faces at the window.

"Let's put on the TV," said Andy.

"OK," agreed Tom. "What time is it? Eight o'clock? Let's see what's on." He got up to turn on the TV. And that's when we heard something. Footsteps. Slow, heavy footsteps. They were walking up the porch steps at the back of the house.

"Who—who's that?" said Andy.

Tom and I didn't know. The footsteps started to walk along the back porch—clump, clump, clump—like someone wearing heavy boots. The footsteps reached the back door. We waited for someone to knock. But the footsteps kept walking. Clump, clump, clump.

Tom and I looked at each other. We thought of faces at the window and howls in the night. But these were footsteps. They went across the porch and down the steps at the other end. Clump, clump, clump. Then there was silence.

"We should see who it is," said Tom.

"Yes, we should," I agreed.

We didn't want to, but we slowly opened the back door and stepped outside.

Andy followed us. It was cold and dark outside. There was no one there. No one at all. "I want to go back inside," said Andy.

"Yes," I said. I took her hand. "Come on. There's nothing here."

Andy and I went inside. Tom stayed on the back porch, peering out into the yard. Tom's braver than I am, I thought. I wouldn't have stayed out there.

And then I wished I had stayed at the back of the house. Because, where Andy and I were, at the front of the house, a face appeared at the window.

Chapter 3

A Face at the Window

I screamed. I couldn't help it. It was a strange, out of focus, blurry face, and it scared me to death!

"Tom!" screamed Andy. "Tom! There's someone here!"

The face disappeared from the window. We heard Tom's footsteps running around the side of the house. Then we heard him yell. There were noises outside, like people running and falling and struggling. A dog barked. Then Tom shouted, "Issy! Andy! Come out here!"

We ran out the front door. There were three figures struggling in the long grass. Tom, a big dog, and the girl we'd seen the first day we came here. "Jenna!" I said. "It's that girl, Jenna!"

When the three of us surrounded her, Jenna stopped struggling. Her face looked very strange—scary and out of focus. She had an old stocking pulled over it.

"It was *you* at the window!" I said. Tom and I were really angry. But Andy, once she was over her fright, only seemed puzzled. "Why would you want to scare us like that?" she asked Jenna.

Jenna looked a bit ashamed of herself. She pulled the stocking off. "I'm sorry you were frightened," she said to Andy.

"But *why?*" insisted Andy.

"Well," said Jenna, "all the kids use this house for a clubhouse. If someone's living here, we can't use it anymore. I thought maybe I could scare you away."

"So you did the graffiti?" I asked.

Jenna nodded. "The other kids did it, too," she said.

"Then maybe you'd like to help clean it up?" invited Tom.

Jenna suddenly grinned at him. "Seems fair," she said.

We went inside and looked at the graffiti. "I'll get the other kids to help," said Jenna.

"What I don't understand," I said slowly, "is how you could make that footsteps noise on the back porch and then get around the house fast enough to look in the front window."

Jenna stared at me. "Footsteps?" she said. "I didn't make any footsteps."

"Yes, you did!" I said. "On the porch. And there was no one there."

"But I didn't do it," said Jenna. And we could tell she wasn't lying.

Chapter 4

Following the Footsteps

If Jenna hadn't made the footsteps, who had? We were determined to find out.

Mom and Dad came back with the pizzas. They were pleased to see Jenna—they thought we were making friends. And I suppose we were.

The next day, Jenna brought some kids over. They helped clean the graffiti off the walls. They were nice kids, and the house looked a little better. Not much—but a little. None of those kids had made the footsteps noise. At least, they said they hadn't. It was a mystery.

And we wanted to solve it.

So, that night, just before eight o'clock, Tom and Andy and I made sure we were in the kitchen. Jenna arrived on her bike, with Alexander trotting beside her. And we waited.

The footsteps came. Just as they had before, they walked slowly up the side steps and along the porch. Clump, clump, clump. As they reached the back door, we opened it wide. And there was no one there. The footsteps went down the steps at the other end.

The next night, we were waiting again. But this time we were outside on the porch. We argued about it. Tom and Jenna were all for it. I wasn't sure. Andy wasn't happy at all.

"The footsteps won't like it," she said. But at eight o'clock we were all there, watching and waiting.

"Maybe they won't come if we're out here," said Andy hopefully.

But they did. Up the steps, along the porch. Clump, clump, clump. Then down the steps at the end of the porch. We all *heard* the footsteps—but there was absolutely nothing there to see.

It was scary. None of us liked it, but Alexander absolutely hated it. He cowered and whined. As soon as the footsteps started, he tried to drag Jenna away. When they'd gone, he was shivering.

"Hey, old boy," said Jenna. "It's only a noise. Nothing there to hurt us."

Andy wasn't so sure. "Maybe Alexander knows better than we do," she said.

We were waiting again the next night.

This time, Jenna and Tom tried to follow the footsteps. After they passed us—clump, clump, clump—Tom and Jenna walked along behind them. Alexander was really upset. Finally, I opened the kitchen door, and Alexander hid inside.

Tom and Jenna followed the footsteps down the steps at the end of the porch. At the bottom, the footsteps stopped. So did Tom and Jenna. "Can't tell where they go," they said. "They just stop."

"We can't follow them then," I said. "Maybe we'll never figure this out."

"Maybe not," said Jenna, "but maybe we will."

"What do you mean?" asked Andy.

But Jenna wouldn't say.

Chapter 5

Something Strange and Cold

Jenna was back again the next night.

Mom and Dad thought we were playing a board game in the kitchen. After a day's hard work on the house, they were happy just to flop into chairs and fall asleep watching TV. Tonight, though, they had a visitor. One of the local policemen, Sergeant Martinez, had stopped by to say hello.

"Great job you're doing," he said. "This house needs looking after. It's been empty for twenty years, ever since the trouble . . ."

"What trouble?" asked Mom quickly.

Sergeant Martinez looked as if he'd said more than he meant to. "Oh, nothing much," he said. "A girl ran away from home. Caused a bit of a stir at the time."

He got up to go. "Nice to have a family here again," he said. "Be seeing you!"

Mom and Dad settled down to watch TV—they'd be asleep in no time. I don't think they'd have been so relaxed if they had known we were planning to confront a ghost. But that's what Jenna had in mind.

"I'm going to stand right in front of the footsteps," she said. "That'll make them stop!"

"Do you think that's a good idea?" I said. "I mean, it's one thing to watch for them . . . "

"But to actually interfere with them," said Tom. "I don't know . . ."

Jenna grinned at him. "Scared?"

Tom didn't like Jenna saying he was scared, but he wasn't going to back down. "Yes," he said. "Yes, I am. And if you had any sense, you would be, too. You have no idea what you're messing around with here."

"Tom's right," I said. "Don't do it."

Jenna grinned again. "Watch me!" she said.

When the footsteps started, we were waiting. They came up the steps. They passed the kitchen door. Alexander was inside, behind the door. He still hated the footsteps. Clump, clump, clump. As the footsteps approached, Jenna moved. Andy grabbed her sweater, but Jenna tugged herself free. She gave Andy a grin—then she stood right in the path of the footsteps.

The footsteps never paused. They kept coming—clump, clump, clump—right up to Jenna. Tom and Andy and I held our breath. And the footsteps went on. We couldn't believe it. They went right *through* Jenna! And as the footsteps passed through her, Alexander gave a long howl from the kitchen.

The footsteps continued—clump, clump, clump—down the steps. Then, silence.

Jenna was standing quite still. We rushed over to her. "Are you all right?" we asked. "What did it feel like? Are you all right?"

Jenna was looking very strange. "I'm all right," she said. "At least I think I'm all right. It just felt cold. Really cold." Suddenly she shivered. "I'm still really cold."

"No wonder you're cold," said Mom's voice from the kitchen. "It's freezing out there. Come inside, for goodness sake! And why is Alexander so upset?"

Poor Alexander was shivering under the table.

"You all look cold," said Mom. "Close the door. I'll make some hot chocolate. Jenna, it's getting late. Would you like to stay for the night? I'll phone your parents."

We thought that would be a good idea. Jenna was still looking very strange. But she was determined to go home. She drank her hot chocolate—though I noticed she left half of it—and then went to get her bike.

She rode off, Alexander beside her. He seemed pleased to get away.

Andy looked after them. "I wish she had stayed," she said.

Chapter 6

The Other Girl

We were having breakfast the next morning when Sergeant Martinez knocked at the door. "I'm investigating an accident," he said. "Did you see or hear anything unusual last night?"

Tom and Andy and I looked at each other. "Not an *accident*," we said.

"I'm sorry to say a girl was hit by a car near here last night," Sergeant Martinez said. "We *think* she was hit by a car. Must have been a hit-and-run."

Mom's face went white. "Was it Jenna?" she asked.

"I'm afraid so," Sergeant Martinez said. "Her parents said she was here. It must have happened on her way home."

"Is she . . . ?" I said. I was too scared to go on.

"Is she all right?" Mom asked.

"She was badly injured," Sergeant Martinez said, "but the hospital says she'll be all right."

"Thank goodness!" Mom said.

"What happened?" asked Dad.

"No one knows," said Sergeant Martinez. "A driver going home found Jenna lying by the side of the road." He paused. "The strange thing is, it was almost at the same place where the other girl was hit."

"What other girl?" I asked.

Sergeant Martinez looked uncomfortable. "I didn't tell you the whole story the other night," he said. "The girl who ran away— well, she had an argument with her father. She took off on her bike. It got late. He waited and worried . . . "

Tom looked up quickly. "Did the father walk up and down the porch?"

"I don't know. He might have," said Sergeant Martinez. "Why?"

"Oh, no reason," said Tom. "Go on."

"Well, he got in his car and went to look for her. He was driving very fast. Apparently the girl felt bad about the argument and was riding home. He didn't see her, and his car hit her—then turned over." Sergeant Martinez shook his head sadly.

"Both of them were killed," he said, "just about where Jenna was found." He paused. "And Jenna was lucky she *was* found. The local librarian was driving home, and Jenna's dog ran out at his car, barking and howling. The librarian knew the dog, so he pulled over and then found Jenna. Otherwise, she might have been there all night."

"And then?" asked Tom.

"It wouldn't have been good for Jenna," said Sergeant Martinez.

I felt sick. Andy started to cry.

Chapter 7

We'll Never Know

Tom and Andy and I went to see Jenna in the hospital. She looked awful. One arm was in a cast, and there was an intravenous drip in her other arm. But she managed a smile.

"What *happened*?" we asked.

Jenna was still sleepy and confused. "They say a car hit me," she said. "But I don't remember a car. And they say my bike isn't damaged, either. All I remember is feeling cold—really cold—all of a sudden. So cold! It was just like . . ." She shivered.

"Like the footsteps," said Andy softly.

"Yes," said Jenna. "Just like the footsteps."

This time, we all shivered. Then we told her about the other accident, all those years ago.

Jenna was in the hospital for a couple of weeks. She's out now, the cast is off, and she's almost OK again.

We still hear the footsteps. Every night they come up the steps to the back porch, walk along the porch, and then down the steps to the backyard. Clump, clump, clump. But now, we leave them alone.

I feel so sorry for that father—if that's who it is—waiting and worrying.

We'll never know if the footsteps really had anything to do with what happened to Jenna.

But we don't mess with the footsteps. And the footsteps don't mess with us.

About the Author

Pamela Rushby

Pamela Rushby has worked in advertising, as a preschool teacher, and as a freelance writer. She is currently a television writer and producer.

Pamela has written over 30 books for children. She lives with her husband, two children, a three-legged cat, and six visiting wild turkeys that peck at the back door for handouts.

She is passionately interested in children's books, television, ancient history, and Middle Eastern food. Although Pamela likes writing about ghosts, she has never met one personally.

About the Illustrator

Kevin Burgemeestre

Kevin illustrates books and prepares collages for a magazine. When he illustrates with ink, Kevin uses a dip-in mapping pen in a loose, friendly manner. For his colored illustrations, he works in either watercolor with soft washes, or strong color applied with sponges. Kevin's collages reflect his passion for movies and cubism, and sometimes end up as sculptures.

Kevin works out of his own studio, which he shares with his enormous collection of car magazines, and his young son, Jim, drawing, drawing, drawing . . .